Sunrise Island

A Story of Japan and Its Arts

Sunrise Island
A Story of Japan and Its Arts

BY CARELLA ALDEN

The Metropolitan Museum of Art,
Gift of Mrs. Henry J. Bernheim, 1945

Detail of picture on page 44

Based on the Japanese production in the
series for young people, Art Entertainments,
presented at The Metropolitan Museum of Art.

PARENTS' MAGAZINE PRESS • NEW YORK

*To my mother, whose stories introduced me to
distant lands and peoples and to times long past.
May this book introduce you to Japan.*

The poems *Spring* by Issa, *Autumn* by Jōsō, and *Winter* by Bashō, on pages 54 and 55,
are from *Haikai and Haiku,* published by The Nippon Gakujutsu Shinkokai, Tokyo;
the poem *Summer* by Onitsura, on page 54, is from *An Introduction to Haiku* by Harold
G. Henderson. Copyright ©1958 by Harold G. Henderson. Reprinted by permission of
Doubleday and Company, Inc.

CONTENTS

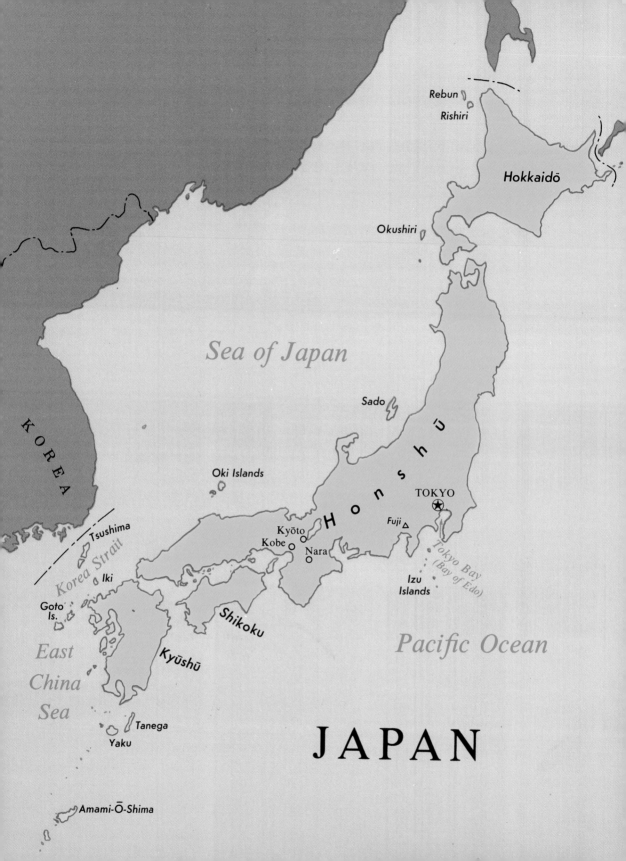

CHAPTER ONE

THE BIRTH OF JAPAN

The land of Japan is made up of four main islands with many small islands around them. The northern island is Hokkaidō. The largest one is Honshū. The smallest one is Shikoku. The southern island is Kyūshū.

Like many lands, Japan has its myths. The most famous one tells of the birth of Japan. In the beginning there was only heaven and earth. Beneath the "plain of high heaven" the earth "floated like oil, moving like a jelly fish." Then one day there appeared on the earth the sprout of a weed. From the weed was born the Eternal-Ruling-Lord. From him came the High-Producing-God and the High-Producing-Goddess. Over many, many years other gods and goddesses were born.

In Japan, gods and goddesses are called *kami* which means "beings more highly placed." Finally two were commanded to go down to earth. Their names were Izanagi and Izanami. They were to bring forth order and "give birth to the drifting land." A sword was given to Izanagi as a symbol of authority. He also carried a spear.

Izanagi and Izanami
on the Floating
Bridge of Heaven

Izanagi and Izanami descended on the Floating Bridge of Heaven. As they neared the earth they were surrounded by mist rising from the water. Izanagi took his spear and tried to sweep the mist away so that they might see, but the spear seemed useless. Then, as they reached the bottom of the Floating Bridge, Izanagi thrust his spear into the water. When he drew it out, salt water had formed into large drops on the spear. As the drops fell back into the sea, they became a tiny island. From the Floating Bridge of Heaven, Izanagi and Izanami stepped onto the first island of Japan. There they became man and wife.

From Izanagi and Izanami came all the islands of Japan. They gave birth to the spirits of the sea and mountains, the trees and rivers, and the spirits of the four seasons. They brought forth too the Storm God, Susano-o, and most important, his sister the Sun Goddess, Amaterasu. Amaterasu was very beautiful and her brilliance shone over the whole earth.

But a time came when Amaterasu and her brother Susano-o had a terrible quarrel. When it was over Amaterasu hid herself in a heavenly cave and would not come out. All the world lay in darkness. To try to get her to come out and shed her light again, the gods and goddesses gathered in front of her cave with magic charms. One of the charms was a bronze mirror decorated with evergreen branches. Among the branches were curved jewels. A bonfire burned to give them light, and cocks waited to announce a new dawn.

The earliest mirrors were made of
highly polished bronze. The backs
of the mirrors were often decorated.

Then one of the goddesses, named Uzume, wearing a charm of bamboo grasses in her hair, began to dance on a wooden tub. At this, everyone began to laugh so loudly that Amaterasu's curiosity got the better of her. She peeked out of her cave to see what was happening. The instant she did so, a god quickly pulled her away from the cave's entrance, while another god held a second mirror up to her face. As the Sun Goddess looked into the mirror she thought she saw another goddess. Believing this goddess was trying to take her place, Amaterasu promised never again to hide her warmth and brilliance from the earth.

Amaterasu is very important in Japanese history for, according to legend, it was her great-great-grandson, Jimmu-Tennō, who, 660 years before the birth of Christ, became the first ruler, or emperor, of Japan. From Jimmu-Tennō have come all the rulers of Japan. The three sacred emblems of these emperors are a sword, a mirror, and a curved jewel.

Courtesy, Sidney B. Solomon,
Cooper Square Publishers
Photograph by Philip Evola

Woodcut by Yeitaku

CHAPTER TWO

JAPAN'S EARLIEST ART

Over the centuries, when Japan was known as Yamato, meaning "mountain-guarded," people moved from Korea to Japan. They brought with them new ways of farming and building. They also knew how to cast objects in bronze. The Koreans had learned these things from the Chinese. The Japanese quickly learned them, too. The rich tones of bronze bells were heard for the first time in Japan. The bells were often decorated.

Archaeologists, digging in ancient burial mounds, have found clay objects made in a native Japanese style. Such sculpture is called *haniwa*. It was the custom to place around graves things the dead had used often during their lives or had prized highly.

The Metropolitan Museum of Art,
Rogers Fund, 1918

Bronze Japanese temple bell

The Cleveland Museum of Art,
The Norweb Collection

Clay horse

CHAPTER THREE

PRINCE SHŌTOKU
AND THE CITY OF NARA

About a thousand years after Emperor Jimmu-Tennō, Japan's first great hero lived. His name was Shōtoku Taishi, or Prince Shōtoku. As a boy he was a very bright student. When he was grown he wrote rules of behavior for emperors, nobles, and the people. The rules were based on justice and respect for all. Because he loved art—all things beautiful—he encouraged the arts. But most of all, Prince Shōtoku was responsible for Buddhism becoming the main religion of the country.

The religion of Buddhism began in India. A very rich prince named Siddhartha Guatama, who lived about the time of Jimmu-Tennō, left his father's palace in India to go out into the world and help the poor. His teachings became a religion and so his followers called him Buddha, "The Enlightened One." Buddhism spread to China and Korea and then Buddhist monks brought the religion to Japan.

This bronze Buddha
was made in India
in the 6th century.

EVENTS IN THE LIFE OF PRINCE SHŌTOKU

The baby prince with his parents.

Events in the life of Prince Shōtoku became popular subjects for artists to paint.

In Japan, Prince Shōtoku is remembered as a temple builder and a man of culture. At a place called Nara he encouraged Buddhist priests to build temples and to make the city a place of learning. In the year 710 Nara became the first capital of Japan and the place where the emperor and his family lived.

The prince racing with a friend in a "stone and bow" contest.

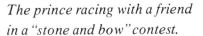

16

As Shōtoku grew to manhood, violence broke out. It was caused by
people who believed in two different religions. A chapel was burned
and a religious sculpture was thrown into a canal (upper right).

Prince Shōtoku became a great speaker on many subjects. One
night after he spoke, it is said, "Lotus petals fell two or
three feet in length." In the background little Buddha heads
seem to be peeking through the trees to see the miracle.

17

*The prince watches the sculptor
at work in a palace workshop.*

Courtesy, Japan National Tourist Organization

*The largest bronze statue in the world
is in an ancient temple at Nara.
Called the Daibutsu Buddha, it is
painted gold, and is almost ten
times the size of the average man.*

18

*The Metropolitan Museum of Art,
Gift of Mrs. John D. Rockefeller, Jr., 1942*

*A very fine gift might have been
a bronze lion much like this one.
It was made at that time, during
the T'ang dynasty in China.*

To Nara came important travelers from China who
brought with them beautiful gifts for the emperor and
priests. And the name of the country was changed from
Yamato to Nippon, which means "place of sunrise."

The kind of beauty and wealth seen at Nara was not the
kind enjoyed everywhere in the land. Most of the people
were peasants and the only beauty they knew was in
nature, in the mountains and lakes, the rivers and forests.
The wealth was in the hands of the landowners. These
great landowners with their families and relatives were
called "clans." But the clans could not exist without the
peasants who grew the rice.

Rice was the main food of the people. It was also used
for money. Almost everything was paid for with rice,
including taxes. Rice was stored against drought, valued
as gifts, honored in stories, and sung about in songs.

CHAPTER FOUR

SHINING LACQUER
AND PAINTED SCROLLS

After seventy-five years, an emperor named Kwammu moved the capital from Nara to a place called Heian-kyō, "Capital of Peace." It later became known as Kyōto. Over the years temples with lovely gardens were built. The temples and the palace of the emperor became filled with art treasures. Some were made of lacquer.

Like many of Japan's arts, the making of lacquer was learned from the Chinese. After a while, though, by developing new methods, the Japanese reached a very high standard of their own.

Lacquer is a varnish made from the sap of a special tree. Fine lacquer-ware takes a long time to make. Many coats are applied to the pieces, which are usually made of wood. Each coat of lacquer is dried in moist air before the next coat is put on. Lacquer-ware is often decorated with silver or gold, shell, mother-of-pearl, and silver or gold dust.

A lacquer writing box

Courtesy, Seattle Art Museum

Deer scroll by Sōtatsu. An ink painting with calligraphy

And just as lacquer artists developed their own styles for decorating lacquer, so too did Japanese painters, in time, develop their own styles of painting.

Instead of painting on canvas, as Western artists do, Japanese painters paint on paper or silk. They use ink or water colors, but not oil. This is because, like the Chinese, their painting developed out of their calligraphy. Calligraphy means beautiful writing, or penmanship. The Chinese and Japanese have always written the characters of their languages with brush and ink. Their ink is made of lampblack, or soot, and their watercolors are from powdered earths and minerals.

Japanese pictures are painted on scrolls. The vertical, up and down, scroll that hangs on a wall is called a *kakemono.*

Portrait of Chigo Daishi: A Japanese legend tells of a priest who, when a child, dreamed he talked with Buddhist gods. In the late 1200s an artist chose the legend as the subject for a painting. In colors, on silk, he pictured the small boy in prayer, kneeling on a lotus pedestal.

A story-telling form of painting is the handscroll. A handscroll is called a *makimono,* pictures that run horizontal, across. A *makimono* is unrolled from right to left. Some are very long. An artist known as Toba Sojō painted one that has become very famous.

2.

The monkey pretended he was a priest.
He made the rabbit bring him food.

*SCENES FROM
THE CHOJU GIGA OR
SCROLL OF ANIMALS*

1. *The water was fine,
   so the animals went
   for a swim. The
   monkeys took a bath.*

CHAPTER FIVE

ART FOR THE WARRIOR

For several hundred years, the real power behind the emperors was a very rich clan named Fujiwara. Then a time came when greed and dishonesty gripped the country like a dragon. War broke out between two rival clans. Each clan wanted to destroy the Fujiwaras and gain control of the Court for itself. The final victor was a man named Minamoto-no-Yoritomo. In 1192, the emperor, to restore order to his land, bestowed on Yoritomo the title of *Shōgun,* Commander-in-Chief.

Yoritomo made his place of command in the village of Kamakura near present-day Tōkyō. He formed a new kind of government called the *Bakufu.* It was a military

Portrait of Minamoto-No-Yoritomo. In Yoritomo's time, it was popular for important people to have their portraits painted. He was painted in colors, on silk, in his ceremonial robes. The sword is his symbol of authority. This is a masterpiece of Japanese portrait painting.

27

The flame-colored braid of this suit of armor identifies it as having belonged to a member of one of the five princely families of Japan. It contains 4,500 scales, 1,000 rivets, and 265 yards of braid.

government. To keep it strong and maintain peace, Yoritomo created a highly skilled army. Its warriors became the famous *samurai,* meaning "one who serves." With the samurai came the art known as military art.

Japanese body armor was made of small steel and leather scales. The scales were lacquered to protect them from the weather. Each scale was covered with silk braid and then they were laced together in rows.

A fierce mask of lacquered metal was worn for three reasons: it protected the face; it kept the helmet in place by being fastened to it; it was supposed to scare the enemy.

The helmet base is a metal bowl of carefully shaped pieces riveted together. The neck defense, made like the body armor, is removable. Japanese armor is highly decorated with silver and gilded metal.

The samurai's weapons? Well, he fought with arrows and a very long bow but his other weapon was far more important to him. Ever since the time of the early myths, the sword had stood for authority and was considered sacred. Samurai swords were made with religious ceremony and carried with religious faith. Each samurai had two, one longer than the other. They were so sharp it is said they could "cut through a pile of copper coins without nicking the blade." It took a samurai a long time to learn how to handle such fine, expensive swords.

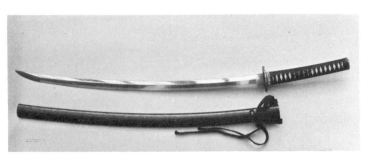

The Metropolitan Museum of Art, Bequest of Giulia P. Morosini, 1932

Samurai sword. The handle of a sword is called the "hilt." It is carried in a scabbard.

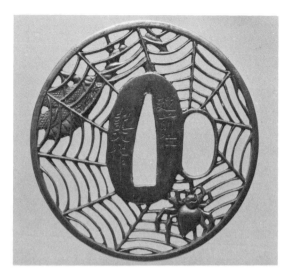

A sword guard. It goes between the hilt and the blade.

For these handsome weapons equally fine mountings were needed. A special art form began. Artists created the designs. Then expert craftsmen produced them in various metals. These mountings are called sword "furniture." Some of them are as well known in Japan as famous paintings. The pieces were made so that they could be easily removed from the blade. A samurai might own several sets. The most elaborate ones were used only for ceremonial occasions.

For the next 675 years the emperors of Japan, the descendants of the Sun Goddess, had little power. Like Amaterasu, they seemed to be hiding. But they were still considered divine and the people continued to worship them. The real power was in the hands of the shōguns, and the samurai became the heroes of the young boys of Japan.

A ceremonial sword

Tales of the samurai live on today in Japanese stories and art.
This is a detail from a painting on a pair of six-fold screens.

CHAPTER SIX

TEA AND GARDENS

A Chinese legend tells of a Buddhist monk who fell asleep while he was praying. To punish himself he cut off his eyelids and threw them on the ground. At the place where they fell, tea bushes grew. When tea was brought to Japan by monks, Zen Buddhist priests drank it to keep from falling asleep. Zen is a sect, or form, of Buddhism that stresses quiet thinking.

In Japan there once lived a Zen priest named Shukō. As a priest he enjoyed doing his thinking in lovely quiet surroundings. As an admirer of art, he enjoyed drinking tea from beautiful porcelain cups. At the same time there lived a shōgun named Ashikaga Yoshimasa. He, too, was a Zen Buddhist but he was also a great patron of art. It was natural for these two men to become close friends. Then Shukō had an idea. A ceremony created for drinking tea! If tea could be served beautifully and drunk from fine cups in a peaceful setting it might be very restful for people.

In Kyōto, an ancestor of Yoshimasa had built a monastery, or religious house, known as the Golden Pavilion. Yoshimasa had built one to rival it called the Silver Pavilion. In a garden nearby he had a little room

Courtesy, Japanese National Tourist Organization

The Golden Pavilion (top) and The Silver Pavilion (bottom)

Tea ceremony set

built just for drinking tea. It was very plain. Its only decoration was a very fine painting. When everything was perfect he invited a few friends in for tea-tasting. Before long they found themselves admiring the handsome tea things and thinking about the beauty in the painting.

Everyone came to love *cha-no-yu,* the tea ceremony, and the custom became so popular that teahouses with tearooms were built in gardens all over Japan.

Gardens were as important to the Japanese as their homes. Designing a garden was an art. The object was to have it appear as if the viewer were looking at a landscape painting come to life. To get this effect, the most beautiful ones, which only the rich could afford, were designed by the most famous painters of the day. A special type of Japanese garden is called a sand garden.

One of the painters employed by the shōgun Yoshimasa was named Sō-ami. A masterpiece by Sō-ami is a tiny sand garden adjoining the teahouse of a temple in Kyōto.

The Metropolitan Museum of Art,
Gift of John D. Rockefeller, Jr., 1941

A sand garden is a contrast between light and dark. When painters designed them, they had in mind a painting in black ink on white paper.

The white sand is carefully raked to represent water. The rocks on the "water" are "islands." The ones in the corner are "mountains." A slab forms a bridge that connects the "mountains" to an "island." It often took a painter a long time to find just the right shape of rocks he wanted to use. He never cut them, for that would be destroying nature. One never walks in a sand garden. It is intended to be seen as a painting is. Often it can stir your imagination. You can create stories in your mind about the "islands" and the "lofty peaks" or perhaps tales of ships that sail on the "sandy sea."

Japan Air Lines Photo

A sand garden in Kyōto

CHAPTER SEVEN

SHIPS AT SUNRISE ISLAND

Not many years after Sō-ami designed that sand garden, real ships were sailing over the oceans of the world. In European history the period is called the Age of Exploration. In Japan it was a period of change and progress. Great riches and great poverty had brought civil wars again. Three men, each in turn, finally united all the peoples of the four main islands. One of them was Toyotomi Hideyoshi.

Courtesy of His Majesty, the Emperor of Japan

Westerners in Japan. A screen painting of a ship in a Japanese port, painted in colors on gilded paper.

During these times ships from Portugal, Spain, and the Netherlands had arrived in Japan. The holds of the great galleons were filled with goods from Europe, China, the Indies, and islands of the Pacific. Among other things, they brought firearms, which the Japanese had never seen.

Hideyoshi knew that Japan could not become an important country on farming alone so he welcomed trade with these countries. Japanese and Chinese goods flowed into Europe. Sailors returning home told tales of the lands in the East that rivaled *The Arabian Nights.* It is from the Dutch that the name Japan came into being. For many years the Chinese and Koreans called Nippon "Jih-pen," their words for "Sunrise Island." The Dutch pronounced it "Jap-an" and so to the Westerner it became Japan.

The Metropolitan Museum of Art,
Rogers Fund, 1957

A six-fold screen showing foreign merchants,
painted in colors on paper.

CHAPTER EIGHT

CASTLES AND PALACES

With foreign trade came prosperity. For the first time a middle-class society arose. And with the wealth of the high military officers there came a new kind of architecture. It is called castle architecture.

Castles were fortresses designed for the army within them to protect the land and its people. Himeji, "The White Heron," at Kobe is a castle with high stone walls surrounded by a moat.

Courtesy, Consulate General of Japan, N.Y.

Today, Himeji Castle stands as if it were a sentinel from ancient times guarding the Inland Sea.

Nijō Palace, Kyoto

Nijō castle in Kyōto, built by the Shōgun Tokugawa Ieyasu, has within its walls a beautiful palace. A palace is where the commander of the castle lived, in this case the shōgun. These castles and palaces were built on a scale never before seen in Japan. Their rooms and halls were very large. On the walls of Nijō palace can be seen a new development in painting, called decorative art. Painters

Interior of Nijō Palace

created large, bold, richly colored designs with gold and silver leaf as background. This gave a shining, luminescent, or pearly, effect. Gold dust was often used for clouds and strips of gold or silver for details. Sliding panels served as walls. When they were pushed back more light came in. The artist also decorated folding screens. Screens were used to partition off a room.

Just as there were Court painters to the emperors, there were official painters to the shōguns. Hideyoshi was a friend to many artists. He built temples, teahouses, and gardens. He had a new palace built for an emperor in Kyōto. In Kyōto too, he had a mansion built for himself and a castle he named "Peach Hill." He filled both with art by the finest painters, lacquerers, wood carvers, and metal workers in the land. He not only paid large sums to the artists for their work but rewarded them with honors. In Japan, Hideyoshi's name lives on today as a great leader, statesman, and patron of the arts.

The Metropolitan Museum of Art,
Louisa E. McBurney Gift Fund, 1953

One of a pair of six-fold screens with iris and bridge.
The painting is done on paper.

CHAPTER NINE

THE FLOATING WORLD

When Hideyoshi died, Tokugawa Ieyasu became shōgun. Though he stayed often at Nijō palace, he chose for his place of government a village called Edo. It was on the shore of a large bay.

Years before, when the first foreign ships landed in Japan, Catholic priests had come to bring their religion to the Japanese people. By the time Ieyasu's grandson became shōgun, it was feared that the Catholic religion had become too strong in Japan. There was also fear of possible invasion from abroad. The shōgun, therefore, ordered all foreigners to leave. Except for a few Dutch and Chinese, Japan closed its doors to the world. They remained closed for over two hundred years.

All during that time there was peace and much progress. The village of Edo grew into a city. It became not only the center of business but also of art and learning.

By the 1700s the large middle-class society had time for leisure and entertainment. There were boating parties and picnics. People sang and danced. They listened to music. And everyone, children and grownups, loved the puppet shows. There were many festivals too, for each month

Boating

Japanese puppets are among the finest in the world.
During this time the very best writers in Japan
wrote stories for the puppets to act out.

*The "tobi" were house builders and firemen. They performed for money.
If the owner of each house did not give them anything, next time his house
needed repair or caught fire, the tobi just wouldn't come.*

*Dolls that once belonged to grandmothers
and great grandmothers were brought out to be
admired during the Festival of Dolls in March.*

*During the Festival of Boys in May,
a large fish, the carp, flew in front of every
house where a boy lived. The carp is a symbol
of strength.*

honored something or someone. In January the *tobi* went around to the houses and entertained the owners with their tumbling. March was for girls. May was for boys.

Several hundred years before this time, the first theater entertainment had begun. It was called Nō, meaning "the art of movement." Prose, poetry, music, singing, and dancing, all were a part of Nō. The plays were short, so several were given at one time. They told stories of ghosts, favorite legends, or sometimes described an historical event. All the characters in the plays, including the women, were played by men. And no matter what part they played, all the actors wore masks.

Nō was given only for members of the royal Court, the very rich, and high ranking people in the military. It is said that Nō grew out of a sacred temple dance based on the one that Uzume danced in front of Amaterasu's cave.

The Metropolitan Museum of Art,
Gift of the Kokusai Bunka Shinkokai, 1935

Model of Nō stage

Kabuki actor

Courtesy of The Art Institute of Chicago

Kabuki Theater

Now, during this later period, there was the Kabuki.
Kabuki was to the middle-class society what Nō was to the
upper class. Like Nō it combined acting, singing, dancing,
and music. But the plays were much longer and far more
elaborate. Also, like Nō, only men acted in them. But
masks were never worn, so make-up became an art. The
costumes were very rich and beautiful. It took years of
training to become a good Kabuki actor and, by tradition,
sons of Kabuki actors usually followed in their fathers'
footsteps. Both Nō and Kabuki are still performed today.
Kabuki companies have traveled to many parts of the
world including the United States. Everywhere it is
considered one of the most difficult of all the
theater arts.

*Pictures that showed people doing things in everyday life became
very popular. Such pictures are called "genre." Here, girls are
writing and playing games. The artist has painted a screen on a screen...*

*...and this tiger looks so real
you can almost feel his fur.*

With increasing prosperity in the land, the work of artists and craftsmen was more in demand. Besides the shōguns and the military, wealthy merchants were patrons of art too. As a result new painters were discovered who painted in new styles and new schools of painting began.

Whenever working-class people saw such fine paintings they admired them, but they could not afford them. Still, there were pictures they could afford. These were woodcuts.

Woodcuts had been in use for a long time in Japan. But until the 1600s no important painter had ever designed a picture especially for a woodcut print. When the demand for pictures became so great, the painter Moronobu saw an opportunity. He would try to design pictures just for woodcuts. They would be quite different from his paintings, but if he succeeded everyone could afford to own a good picture. He succeeded; and soon other famous painters were following him.

For a woodcut, the artist first paints a picture on paper. This picture is used as a pattern by a cutter, who carves it into a wooden block. The block is covered with ink and the paper is then pressed down on it. When the paper is removed, the picture on it is called a print.

For many years the prints were in black and white. Later they were colored by hand with watercolors. Then, in the 1700s the color print was invented. To make a color print the artist had to make a separate picture for each color. Everything that he wanted in yellow he drew and marked "yellow." Then he made another drawing for the part that he wanted in blue, and so on.

The drawings for the separate colors were sent to a cutter who cut each one on a block of cherry wood. If the artist wanted a picture in six colors, six blocks would be cut. The blocks were sent to a printer. The printer inked each block with its proper color, then carefully pressed a sheet of ivory-colored paper onto the block. When the paper had been pressed over all the blocks, the artist was able to see his finished print.

1. *The cutter, using the picture as a pattern, carves it into a wooden block.*

2. *The block is covered with ink.*

3. *A sheet of paper is pressed onto the block over the ink. (Finished prints are piled up on the side.)*

1.

2.

3.

The Metropolitan Museum of Art,
Bequest of Mrs. H. O. Havemeyer, 1929
The H. O. Havemeyer Collection

Hokusai: The Great Wave Off Kanagawa

From the woodblocks a printer could make many copies. This lowered the cost of a single picture.

Among the finest print designers was the painter Hokusai. One of his masterpieces is from a series he called "The Thirty-six Views of Fuji." Fuji is the sacred mountain of Japan. It is inland from the sea. But in Hokusai's print, "The Great Wave Off Kanagawa," the mountains appear as if they were another wave.

Among the most popular prints were street scenes...

The most popular prints were of street scenes in Edo, famous Kabuki actors, and people having fun.

Since ancient times the Japanese have loved poetry. The most popular form was called *haiku.* Everyone composed the little verses, even emperors. On pages 54 and 55, are a few, illustrated with woodcut prints.

...and Kabuki actors.

53

SPRING
Bud-unfolding; "Spring rain! Spring rain!"
Chant the small birds.

SUMMER
Although I say:
"Come here! Come here!" the fireflies
Keep flying away!

Courtesy, Museum of Fine Arts, Boston,
William S. and John T. Spaulding Collection

Spring: Red-cheeked Bird
and Red Plum Blossoms

The Metropolitan Museum of Art,
Bequest of Mrs. H. O. Havemeyer, 1929
The H. O. Havemeyer Collection

Summer: A Lady and Child at
Night Watching Fireflies

AUTUMN

The young wild duck
Looks as if it were saying:
"I've been down to the bottom and seen everything."

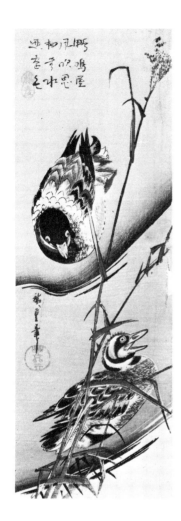

The Metropolitan Museum of Art,
Bequest of Mrs. H. O. Havemeyer, 1929
The H. O. Havemeyer Collection

Autumn: Ducks

WINTER

A winter's day!
On horseback, frozen,
A mere shadow of myself.

The Metropolitan Museum of Art,
Bequest of Henry L. Phillips, 1940

Winter

Fireworks

This time of pleasure in Japan, the boating, picnics,
and festivals, the singing, dancing, and the Kabuki; yes,
even the fun of making up haiku—is called *Ukiyo. Ukiyo*
means "the floating world." "E" means "pictures." So there
came into being the Ukiyo-e school of art—pictures of
the floating world.

CHAPTER TEN

FROM EAST TO WEST

One day a strange sight appeared in the Bay of Edo. On July 8, 1853 a fleet of ships, flying the American flag, sailed toward the port and dropped anchor. The fleet's Commander, Commodore Matthew C. Perry, went ashore. He presented letters to the shōgun and explained

Courtesy, Chicago Historical Society

James G. Evans: Commodore Perry's ships arriving in the Bay of Edo.   57

they were for the emperor from the President of the United States, Millard Fillmore. They requested permission to set up trading posts in Japan. Perry then sailed away, saying he would return in one year to receive the emperor's reply.

When Perry came back, the Japanese gave him gifts of beautiful art objects. Among the American gifts to the Japanese were a small locomotive engine with tracks, farming equipment, a sewing machine, a telegraph set, and a book of Audubon bird pictures.

The doors of Japan opened to the world again. Fourteen years later, in 1867, the many centuries of rule by the shōguns ended. Like the Sun Goddess coming out of her cave to shed light again, the power of government was given back to the emperor. The new ruler, "the descendant of Amaterasu," was fifteen-year-old Mutsuhito.

Mutsuhito moved the capital from Kyōto to Edo. The name of the city was changed to Tōkyō, meaning "Eastern capital." And the period that followed was called *Meiji,* which means "enlightened government."

Ships filled with Japanese goods soon were arriving in ports all over the world. And the art from the East began to influence artists in the West.

James McNeill Whistler: Lady of the Lange Lijsen, 1864

Photograph courtesy The Museum of Modern Art, New York

Frank Lloyd Wright: Coonley House, Riverside, Illinois, 1907-10

Courtesy, Consulate General of Japan, N.Y.

Historic Japanese buildings in the Sankeien Garden in Yokohama

But when you study the arts of Japan, when you read Japanese stories and poems, you notice that one very special thing stands out. It is the Japanese love and respect for the beauty in nature, even if it is only a bird on a leafless branch.

Courtesy of Mr. Sotaro Kubo, Japan

INDEX

(Bold figures indicate illustrations)